Liam,
With God, limitless possibilities!
Thank you for fathuking me
in many ways!

Leo Ndumvere Ezeogu

BOY

HIS DUMBS, HIS LEARNINGS!

LEO EZEOGU

Boy by Leo Ezeogu

ISBN: 9798652473037

ACKNOWLEDGEMENT

This project BOY, has in no small way, enhanced my appreciation for the selflessness of those who consistently reach into you, highlight the gems in you, bring out the best in you, and help you present that best from you, in your best possible way, to your world. Truly, I am now much more grateful for every person that has graced me with the workings of their selflessness, in my few decades of existence. In 1999, a friend of mine – Emeka Edeh, after reading something which I had written on some random piece of paper, advised me to start writing in a notebook to help me preserve my writings better. Thank you Emeka! The truth is, BOY might never have existed if I did not heed to your advice. Not long after creating a journal for my writings then, I began to dream about being published some day! Here we are, twenty plus years later!

Having finished compiling the manuscript for BOY, I had no idea what my next step publishing-wise, would be. Almost immediately, some key contributors to its completion, began to (re) surface in my life. A great support during the 'second phase' of this project was Jude Nwogu – a precious friend of mine. I had only just reconnected with the Nwogus – Jude and Sandra, and in that conversation which lasted hours upon hours, Jude suggested and inspired the 'doodlings' within BOY, and its cover too. Thank you! *De Jude* (igbo accent), we have greater works to do.

Additionally, I am grateful for some priceless pillars in my life, the Townsends (Christina and Dave) who love me non-stop, pray for me non-stop and keep me grateful to God non-stop, ever fulfilling the parents-friends-mentors combo in my life. I am always grateful to, and for you! My personal Mummy – Mrs. Nkechi Okaro, who's streams of wisdom never run dry, thank you so much for the many free life-lessons which you give to me without fail. Revd. Chris Enwerem (my Uncle Rev) the most laidback mighty man that I know, married to one of the homeliest women that I know – Foluso, and father to the most vision-driven children that I know – Comfort, Peace and Praise, thank you for our many conversations, and your chilled wisdom.

There's more! Barrister Chidi Otamiri *thank you for every*! Revd. Liam Hanna, a man who has fathered me in many ways, who also took *some while* to read through BOY in its very raw and miry state, I am so grateful for that *while*, thank you Sir! To my sister Ada – Mrs. Leona A. Aaron (CEO of Leona's Kitchen), the world is waiting for you and *our* kitchen, thank you for your many supports! Chibueze Onyema, Ikenna Agbeze, for the many things you have done and still do for me, thank you! To Chioma Ezeogu – my out of this world cousin, thank you so much for your heart! Last but definitely not the least, to the lovely Brierleys – Sarah and Mark, who funded my food-scholarship while I edited BOY, thank you so very much!

Most of all, I am grateful to my Creator, the Creator of all that is, for His gift of life to me, and for the many blessings which He has brought my way, in and through a variety of humans, many of whom are not mentioned here, albeit unintentionally. ‡

DEDICATION

To that person still living,
  who still dares to think — "I can!",
with the minutest amount of faith,

and resolves to move towards "I can!",
  not minding the burdens borne,
from many fears and fails. ‡

  ◆ 08.06.2020.

INTRODUCTION

Undeniably, I do question the plausibility of my parents, on conceiving me, determining that their son would grow up to be a person quite fascinated with writing, or become one who would even dare to identify himself as a poet. However, I must admit that my parents are very responsible for my adventures so far, with words — written and spoken.

Not that I have known them to be avid poets or writers, my dad as I saw, did more doodling than writing really! On a few occasions though, he did write. My mum never grew tired of talking about the many letters which he wrote her, professing his love for her. Additionally, in the days when stereo-sets operated without remote controls, it was my responsibility to change over the cassette in the cassette-player to the other side or, flip over the vinyl-plate on the turntable whenever it ran out of songs on the side which played. As a result, I sometimes did frequent my dad's stereo-set much more than my dad did, while he listened to the music. More than anything else, this granted me access to his record collection, and subconsciously imbued me with many rhymes from a few renowned lyricists of the seventies and eighties.

My mum, on the other hand, tirelessly sang all that was '*sing-able*' and child-appropriate to me when I was a toddler, and even beyond. I must confess that her voice was just as sonorous as the many vocalists, who sang in the nursery rhymes which bellowed from my dad's stereo. To her innumerable repetitions of nursery rhymes and songs, I sang along, rhymed along, and soon I was inventing my own sing-alongs too.

Indelible in my memory, is my first self-composed, and I mean self-composed – unaided, song. Warning! The venue was a toilet seat, and I was calling out, rather singing out for our make-shift nanny – Chinwe, to help me clean my bum, very well, after doing a number two. This I sang –

> "I have finished,
>   I have finished,
> Chinwe come!
>
> I don't know how to clean
>   my bum, very well,
> I don't know how to clean
>   my bum very well.
>
> I have finished,

I have finished,
Chinwe come!"

Chinwe remembers that song till this day. She reminded me of how I used to disturb her with that song when we last saw ourselves, in 2018 – the fourth decade since its debut. My *bum-cleaning* song was released at the spur of that moment in the early eighties, but the prowess of this child-prodigy was ignorantly trivialised then. Life! Well, life upon life has happened since, and I am still writing and singing poems, decades later.

Interestingly, there are many things which I still cannot do very well. Poetry occasionally feels like one of such things. Especially as I do not know of any poet that has attained to perfection yet. Even great poets do admit that there is always room for improvement. Could words convey perfect poetic expression? Sometimes maybe, but then perfect usually is relative! Therein lies my subliminal but ever-present discomfort with describing myself as either a wordsmith or poet, though a few friends and colleagues dare to call me either or both. Truly, I am still hunting for that ever-elusive perfect poetic expression on the inside of me. Concerning my relationships with words, I do love words! I must confess that the various sequence of emanating sounds during the pronunciation of certain words, do have an almost intoxicating effect on me. Indeed, I joyously relish in the sounding of such words – incongruously. Strangely, that is my truth!

Back to my *bum-cleaning* song, as I started to write the last paragraph, I realised that, until a year or two before I began to consider compiling and writing the poems for this book – BOY, that I had all my life, been singing that same song with the alteration of just two words – *dumbs* for *bum*, and *God* for *Chinwe*.

> "I have finished,
>   I have finished,
> God come!
>
> I don't know how to clean
>   my dumbs, very well..."

Unwittingly, I would embark on whatever it was that I wanted to do, and it was only after my many unsuccessful tries and mistakes, that I would invite God into the picture. At most of such times before the invite, instead of smooth-sailing I would spend excruciating efforts trying to rectify what should have been avoided in the first place. Well, I outgrew singing to Chinwe, and after many *dumbs* – follies heaped on follies, I grew tired of singing "clean my dumbs" to God. Especially as I could learn with His help not to be compulsively dumb anymore. BOY documents some of these *dumbs*, and learnings! ‡

PREAMBLE

So relentless was
  my endeavour to please mankind,
that it cost me my 'God-kind'.
  This dilemma left me
encumbered by my imperfections,
  and lumbered by my insurrections.
I ran away from me, bemoaning a flawed me,
  searching as well as reaching, for a 'flawless' me.

Consequently, I dabbled with,
  and then squabbled over ventures
that enunciated more questions
  within me. This flaming curiosity
within me, yielded more ambiguity.
  I sequestered in frivolities
while my dissatisfactions
  fettered my creativity.
Oh, how these activities
  ate deep into my account — time.

With lamentations as my endless brew,
  and reclination my seamless due,

I redrew, back into myself
  as an indecorous recluse.
Only then did I dare to venture
  beyond the abyss — my soul,
which waxed 'deadish' to me.
  Life had lambasted me!

"Help!" I bellowed,
  and my progression was revealed
my intentions mellowed
  and the transaction appealed.

Then, I realised that my life,
  Had been all about God subtly
wooing me, reading me to me,
  leading me and steadying me.
Furthermore, He was grooming me,
  and growing Himself in me.

My clarity remains infinitesimal
  to the whole scheme of things,
but 'BOY' — a title prompted
  by many immaturities of mine,
attempts to mine from my varied

occasions and reflections,
which contributed to me
   returning to my Source – God. ‡

   ◆ 21.05.2020.

I asked a friend to define a man
  and he was wanting for words.
I asked him to define himself,
  It was an unaccomplished mission. ‡

  ◆ 10.10.2011.

HEFTY YET EMPTY

Hefty yet empty,
  Feigning plenty to reign with empty,
Employing lengthy to engage with empty,
  Fighting deftly to establish empty.
Then the years go by —

Not so hefty but empty,
  Reigning dusty, leaves eyes misty.
Feisty truncates the blossoming of beauty,
  The party serves to distract empty.
Then the years go by —

Eternity summons hefty,
  Clarity buttresses on empty,
Consequentially, weighty is judged by the Almighty,
  Memory serves empty with his haughty.
Now, eternity plays on. ✝

  ◆ 21.03.2014.

LONE LEAF

Untangled from its source,
　Detrimental is its course.

No more function, hence suction.
　The juice, exhausted! The glow, busted!

No renovation, degradation —
　Gory is the story, lost is the glory.

Lone leaf, borne grief. ‡

　◆ Written in 2004.

DEATH VS. LIFE

In death it is
　Madness, blindness
And astonishment of heart,
　That follows the man.

In Christ it is
　Soundness, lightness
And resourcefulness of heart,
　That follows the man.[1] ‡

◆ 02.04.2013.

---

[1] My meditations on Deuteronomy 30:15 – "*See, I have set before you today life and good, death and evil.*", inspired this poem. They led me into contemplations on what death was, and what life (in Christ) was. I found succinct answer in the following verses – Deuteronomy 28.22 – "*The LORD will strike you with wasting disease and with fever, inflammation and fiery heat, and with drought and with blight and with mildew. They shall pursue you until you perish.*", and 2 Timothy 1:7 – "*for God gave us a spirit not of fear but of power and love and self-control.*", and the poem Death vs. Life, was born.

GIFTS

Gifts necessitate lifts,
  Gifts shift and drift
Many, into euphoric bliss.

Gifts fuel progress.
  Gifts create access, halt distress,
They enable success.

Gifts silence rifts,
  Eliminate sifts, and are too thrift
To potentials miss.

Gifts command influence,
  Define ambience, curtain offence,
They serve as reference.

Jesus' gift, did so much more. ‡

  ◆ 13.12.2012.

YOUR MONEY

Are your money tentacles,
  phoney spectacles
or journey cubicles?

Do they sanction obstacles,
  function ridicules
or juncture debacles?

That to which you give,
  With you, that same will live. ‡

  ◆ 30.04.2013.

GAME MODE

You can know the game,
  Have the mind for the game,
Pay the time for the game,
  Have the skills for the game,
Or know the 'whos' of the game.

But only the mind for the game,
  At the time of the game,
The skills in your game,
  Despite who's in the game,
Till the end of the game.

That will win you the game,
  When they better foes in your game. ‡

◆ 11.09.2011.

EITHER OR

Security versus opportunity —
  Both gnaw at my credibility.
Incline to opportunity is my propensity.
  Before I acquiesce, I question durability.

Security constrains my fluidity.
  Opportunity has an unknown finality.
Between options I know mediocrity
  As each reality, demands totality. ‡

  ♦ 24.05.2013.

CONFLICT

Folly is quick to be stern,
   Wisdom is quick to discern!

One will judge based on the wave,
The other won't begrudge if asked, she'll save.

Folly is quick to yearn,
   Wisdom is quick to learn!

One will jump at every alluring idea,
The other will dump if evil features there.

As one they can't reside,
   With one you must abide! ‡

   ◆ 15.11.2012.

RIDDLE

With God nothing is nothing,
  With man nothing is nothing!

With God something is something,
  With man something is something!

Nothing or nothings,
  Something or somethings,
You decide! ‡

  ◆ 09.05.2013.

VACUUM

It is there I know,
   that place with longings insatiable,
   and cries, inaudible.

Inaccessible to pleasantries,
   Inalterable by my disposition,
Inalienable by my person,
   Incalculable in natural dimensions.

Inconceivable by associates,
   Inconsolable by companionship,
Indescribable by words,
   Indestructible by my engagements.

Imperceptible to onlookers,
   Irreplaceable by substitutes,
Insusceptible to variations,
   Inarguable by incongruous logicians.

Indubitably established by my longing.
   I need a filling sourced by
   the Almighty God alone. ✝

• 09.10.2008.

DISTRACTED

My indicators are on,
  Fellowship is lacking.
The predators aren't gone,
  Censorship is packing.

You are hungry, feed!
  Your mind's cloggy, weed!

My negotiation is done,
  The championship's hacking.
Confrontation has shone,
  From membership I'm backing.

You are hungry, feed!
  Your mind's cloggy, weed! ‡

  ◆ 30.05.2013.

ATTITUDE

Gyrating hips, daring stance,
  Exaggerated strides,
Constantly revolving eyes,
  Smirking lips, restless hands,
                    Tapping feet!

The chewing gum had
  Crackled, busted, expanded,
And it still was doing so.

This individual had it in mind
  To come in unannounced, yet
The effect of their entrance
  Was too conspicuous for words,
It was a very noisy silence. ‡

  ◆ 29.05.2008.

ADVERTISING

Announcing the presence,
  Communicating the essence,
Spreading the fragrance by deeds.

Promoting its reverence,
  Reorienting the influence,
Cultivating dependence by seeds.

Circulating cognisance,
  Substantiating relevance,
Encouraging renaissance by feeds.

Advertising – she breeds the need. ‡

  ◆ Written before 2007.

MY MOTIVATION

Invigorating the flame,
  That burns on my inside.
Configurating the turmoil,
  That surrounds my outside.

Blowing my mind,
  Glowing like polished hind.
Flowing no bind,
  Ploughing potentials behind.

Barricading unyieldingness,
  Evading complacency.
Disregarding relatedness,
  Curtailing conspiracy.

Necessitating eruptions,
  That precede accomplishment.
Encapsulating formations,
  That forbid discouragement.

Stretching my zone,
  Fetching my stones.

Sketching to atone,
  Etching ingenuity alone.

Glorifying insignificance,
  Defying conceptions.
Beautifying inconvenience,
  Exalting malfunctions.

Facilitating those strides,
  That waver not in pace.
Dehydrating all personifications
  Of pride, which I brace.

Laying my path,
  Okaying my garth.
Staying to birth,
  Spraying scintillating lath.

Relocating mediocrity,
  Collating vitality.
Dislocating hostility,
  Reinstating impunity.

Coordinating the fire, that

Consumes my entire being.
Reactivating the springs within,
That ideas so genuine bring –

That's the Holy Spirit. ✝

✦ 08.08.2001.

SWAG

Your swag
  Is a body-drag,
If you only brag,
  About a borrowed flag.

Don't be a hag
  With an inimical bag.
Though tongues wag,
  Your tale is their gag.

Your very own swag,
  Can bare God's tag.
Do not exchange your flag,
  For a needless nag or rag. ‡

  ◆ 16.04.2013.

VOICEMAIL

Available? No!

Reachable? Maybe!

Approachable? Yes!

Viable? Leave your name,

and number, and we'll see! ‡

◆ 08.04.2013.

BEGGARLY SNUB

Who can
  This intelligence, explain?

A snobbery that craves and
  Raves for decaying bargains,

Right after the display
  Of his 'dignified' disdain.

Good Lord,
  None of me should complain! ‡

  ◆ 10.08.2013.

PORN

Within porn,
  Lies a horn,
That is worn,
  In mind's torn,
By ills born,
  In rays shone, in her con.

Run! Run! Run! ‡

  ◆ 12.12.2012.

PARANOID

Shame we'll never
   Engage in conversation,

As I wear this
   Impenetrable disposition.

I'm clueless to your
   Intent in this exemption,

Here my every interaction,
   Is a torturous convolution. ‡

   ◆ 12.09.2012.

HANDICAPPED

Those eyes, their cry —

Independence is confined to a wheelchair.
Expression tries to conceal but reveals,
The pain, the drain, the strain.

The wheels, his heels —

An innocent stare, disturbs his wound.
Away he wheels, yet his heart does appeal,
That love, may resolve, to solve.

He drifts from gift —

The hands do rest but not the quest.
Every comment seems to ignite torment,
The sighs of why, still I try.

He knows, to go. ‡

♦ Written in 2004.

RANGER DANGER

Greetings shield analysis.
  Meetings field paralysis.
Fleeting is the prognosis.
  Heating is the symbiosis, soon

Greetings build analysis.
  Meetings include paralysis.
Quitting is the prognosis.
  Pitting is the symbiosis, soon

Greetings will demand analysis.
  Meetings command paralysis.
Beaten will be prognosis.
  Smitten will be symbiosis, soon. ‡

  ◆ 22.05.2013.

DEADISH BOY

Blasé with your allure,
  Unrivalled in your cacophony.
Pressing onwards, you only consolidate —
  Your daftness, your blindness,
Of them you ail, clueless.

Summoned by your lord — lunacy
  The only to whom you've pledged loyalty.
Your exhibitions of gloom do animations play —
  In sameness, in finesse,
But from you, soundness strays.

Deeply ingrained in insecurities,
  Your attacks remain sporadic, uncaused.
Seeing insults in all, you shoot —
  Your bullets, your fillets,
All donated by your lingering shame.

Flaunting your lies, you revel
  In a confidence estranged by you.
Still the key elements of life elude you —
  I mean sincerity, productivity,

Did I hear you say you are living? ‡

♦ 21.08.2011.

REBELS

Bumptious elementaries,
   Name their trajectory.

Riotous contemporaries,
   Claim they are exemplary.

Fractious quandaries,
   Frame their territory.

Piteous inflammatories,
   Flame their legendary.

The result —
   A grievous tragedy! ‡

   ◆ 22.07.2013.

CONGO QUANGO

How vocal, the quango in Congo?
  The rebels parade their jingo.
Many families need a flee, they dare not plea!

For them, publicising the nation's present tango
  Consequentially, will out-sting an immature mango.
As brutal repercussions, shadow all confrontations.

How vocal, the quango in Congo?
  The rebels still parade their jingo.
Many families need a flee, can anyone, free? ‡

  ◆ 04.10.2011.

PRIDE

Socially unbecoming,
  You parade ignoramus,
Leading him homewards,
  Eager for your conjugation.

Stealthily,
You sway through sanity,
  As if you are invincible to view.
Feigning absentia in your rage,
  You think you flee your nemesis — fear.

Socially alarming,
  You deny the qualms in you.
Dwelling on paltry sheets,
  You sanction your fettering. ‡

  ◆ 20.08.2011.

PERFECT, BEWARE!

No flaws,
  Less walls.

No claws,
  Mess stalls.

No laws,
  Dress falls.

Then sin, sin, sin![2] ‡

  ◆ 17.05.2013.

---

[2] Let he who thinks he stands take heed lest he falls – 1 Corinthians 10.12.

ADDICT HABIT

My curse! Lust! I yearn for a union.
  I invest my time, thoughts, and all,
Still nothing but a painful depreciation,
                    that radiates repulsion.

Deed's done and dusted, yet I yearn again,
  Longing for a hug, a snug what more can I do.
I delete everything for no more than a week,
  I'm addicted again — porn, I'm weak

My fuss, ridicule! It belittles me.
  My worth's diminishing daily, friends are gone.
Me — a verified laughingstock, governed by folly's clock.

Sexless, friendless, senseless,
  I am more of a charity-case than I am cool.
So vexing are my errors still, this living repeats,
  Its routine defeats. ‡

    ♦ 10.09.2011.

SHHHHHH!

Shhhhhh!

Impulsive cannot birth submissive.

Shhhhhh!

Emotive cannot rationalise deceptive.

Shhhhhh!

Abusive thrives on ablative.

Shhhhhh!

The operative calls you addictive. ‡

♦ 12.02.2013.

SHY BOY

Jumbles up facts,

   Grumbles at responsibilities,

Tumbles over nothing,

   Fumbles at gatherings,

Crumbles before remarks,

   Stumbles at unseen stones. ‡

   ◆ Written in 2001.

DENIED

The bag of sweets is his,
  The love of sweets is his,
His love is displayed for these,
  His wish is delayed by these —
              the reality.

Loving, wishing, here second
  Having the bag of sweets sectioned.
In desperation, he has beckoned
  But his ownership is not mentioned —
              his mentality.

Yet the bag of sweets is his
  And the love for sweets is his.
Hurts abound by these.
  Thoughts resound from these —
              his reality. ✝

  ◆ 07.05.2013.

FRAUD

Mimicking glorious duties,
  Implementing monstrosities.

Feigning ceremonies,
  Raining acrimonies.

The confusion continues,
  Netting illusion's revenue. ‡

  ◆ 23.05.2013.

GIFT OF GAB

Now your array of words,
   Compete with floral displays.

Branded by your inflexions,
   They are patterned distinctly.

Introducing information with
   A dexterity perfected by you,

Making a fine viewing
   And oozing, a succinct aura. ‡

   ♦ 11.08.2013.

DIPLOMATIC

Inarguably, he said "No!"
Supposing you'd discern
   He intended "Yes!"

When he says "Yes!"
You are to appreciate
   That he connotes "No!"

If you articulate
That he meant "No!"
   He'll say he alleged "Yes!"

If you concur
That he meant "Yes!"
   He'll emphasise "No means no!" ‡

  ◆ 14.08.2013.

PRECIOUS

When facetious
  Merges with spurious.
You'll sure find nebulous,
  And that is insidious.

Forget delicious,
  For within is dangerous.

Never let infectious
  Distance you from cautious.
Nor righteous,
  Certify you as ridiculous. ‡

  ◆ 22.08.2011.

FALSE PROPHET

Prove a lie,
   Ring your bell!
Prove a lie,
   For clientele!

Prove a lie,
   To hearts compel!
Prove a lie,
   Heat their hell!

Still you —

Prophesy,
   And heresies tell!
Prophesy,
   To truth expel! ‡

   ◆ 16.05.2013.

LIES, LIES, LIES!

Lied to by the millions,
   I am swayed to engage in discourse.
But mere words by the trillions,
   Would never redirect cruelty's course. ‡

   ◆ 02.06.2012.

PROBLEM CHILD

Society labels and then you rebel.
  Deep down you yearn to be yourself —
But that you, remains elusive to you.
  So, you numb your senses and perfect pretences,
Vowing to share your conflict with the world.

You give and refuse to heave,
  You give and do not live.

Society cradles and then they saddle,
  Deep down you yearn to be released.
But that person remains undiscovered by you.
  So, you sharpen your reflexes without inferences,
Vowing to reward any potential insult.

You refuse to consult fault,
  You assault by default.

Society furnishes and then punishes,
  Deep down you cry for a refurbishment.
But you think that the only person involved is you.
  So, you stray from reality but not the eventuality,

Vowing to certify your ruin in ignorance.

Now you stay the hope in your day,
  You decay, even as you stray. ✝

  ◆ 20.08.2011.

DOUBT'S SHOUT

Is a confirmation, an affirmation
  That the declaration, was God's revelation?
Is my conclusion, an illusion
  That births delusion, in my seclusion?
Is this information, my motivation
  For seeing limitation, in my destination?
Is my confusion, an intrusion
  That sucks formation, from my confession?
Is my trepidation, a celebration
  For my aggravation, towards humiliation?
Does my omission, spell demotion
  And more commotion, for my duration?
Will an elevation, from depreciation
  Be my realisation in this dispensation? ✝

◆ 08.11.2012.

SELFISH KIND

When kindness demands reciprocation,
  Conscience has attained to insubordination.
For gestures will fuel false indoctrinations,
  Even as wants motivate glorifications.

If your heart flaunts its neutralisation,
  And your pleasures fuel condemnation.
What is the purpose of your revelation?
  I wish to discern other than selfish gyration. ‡

◆ 23.02.2013.

FOOL SCHOOL

No education is fit for a fool,
  Save the rewards of his own folly.
For sometimes, consequence lectures,
  In realms where experience,
                    never ventures.

No contribution is fit for a fool,
  Save the rewards of his own folly.
For sometimes, silence does disqualify,
  The pleasures which his licenses,
                    satisfy.

No aggravation is fit for a fool,
  Save the rewards of his own folly.
For sometimes, the flaws in which he revels,
  Entrap him in the jaws against
                    which he rebels.

No information is fit for a fool,
  Save the rewards of his own folly.
For it is his choice to eventually remain,
  Even though his actions,

perpetually disdain. ‡

◆ 27.09.2012.

IS FAMILY A GONER?

Two pairs of eyes enmesh themselves,
  Ignorant of their individual demands,
Yearning for the warmth of the other's host.
  Eventually, words inspired by sensuality surface.
These are exchanged, and fluids too.

Well, well, well. . .

A new life awakens, unplanned, unannounced.
  Reality dethrones pleasantries, opinions flow.
Seemingly, the best is to start a family.
  A merger ensues, no checks, no affirmations,
Just a product of circumstance.

Well, well, well. . .

Decades later, the crisis begins, rebellion —
  More kids, more chaos, strangers still together.
Longing for an escape, longing for acceptance,
  Running from abandon, their inherent pain
Continually, is their only.

Well, well, well. . .

Adulthood is then imposed on him so naïve,
  On him, who lacks the vital educations of life.
Realising that his foundational notions are false,
  He seeks a reprieve, but none would him receive.
The divorce proceeds to abysmal.

Well, well, well. . .

The decades gone by would never recur.
  The only concrete possession he has is him in now.
His readjustments could take a lifetime.
  In him a question remains —
Will he subject a life to the life he knew?

Well, well, well. . . ‡

  ◆ 04.07.2009.

FLAWED DEMOCRACY

Looting, polluting, rooting, imputing!
  Should all these be synonymous with politics?
Booting, footing, hooting, shooting!
  Strangely, they all merge to form campaign antics.

The lords strategise with their pawns,
  Claiming chattels from blooming lawns.
Leaflets churn, loyalties turn, monies burn,
  With threats made and supports paid, fights dawn.

Blame, inflamed, shame, defamed!
  These intertwine at the aftermath.
Distance, acceptance, defiance, resistance,
  Are concealed to avoid a blood bath.

The affiliation to the throne is now knotty.
  Selfishness corrodes all sense of duty.
Sporadic pleas for national aid become hooty,
  This leaves the commoner wanting for beauty.

Fallacy, injury, penury, tyranny!
  The progression is plain for all to see.

Re-elects, reflects, regrets, rejects!

Who then can save from these pains that be? ‡

◆ 12.12.2011.

SLAVERY

Only a slave
  Repeatedly discusses
The blemish of his master —
  And that in gossip.
For confrontation's umph,
  He cannot muster.

That same slave
  Constantly miss-courses
His growth from his master —
  And that by gossip.
As degradation's umph,
  He surely fosters. ‡

   ◆ 20.07.2013.

RELIVING HURTS

Random alliances result from
  The exploitation of her trust.
Her hurts, binding and blinding her,
  From the precincts of reason.

She flinches at compliments
  And clinches unto sentiments.
Only to be hurt again,
  By 'hellos' from resounding anguish.

Sadly, this living is not known to only she.
  For the unforgiving, it is a guarantee. ‡

  ◆ 19.11.2011.

UNFORGIVENESS

Unforgiveness eats away at
  Hearts which allow her stay —

Notions create commotions,
  Emotions cause demotions,
Confusion births illusion,
  Fruition harbours pollution.

Unforgiveness eats away at
  Hearts which allow her stay —

Solutions greet exclusions,
  Deception merits ascension,
Elation ignites vexation,
  Compulsion sires dysfunction.

Unforgiveness eats away at
  Hearts which allow her stay! ‡

  ◆ 10.10.2012.

HATRED

Hatred has a look,
  Confirmed by the book.
The heart that does her cook,
  Is trapped by her hook.

Her rankings are a fluke,
  She's so easy to juke.
With her, love's a spook,
  She tells of things that shook.

Despite he who you, forsook,
  Or your cache took,
Expel hate from that nook,
  She seconds love in every duke. ‡

   ◆ 08.04.2013.

RUMOUR HUMOUR

Oh, he is! I did and he did so, he is.
  He conclusively is, definitely is.
The validation of my certainty.
  Is the fact that he did, as I did.

And what did he do?

Oh, he did what his type do, I tested he fell.
  He did humour me. He thought I was what I wasn't.
Fool! How disgusting he is.
  Poking, stroking, joking with himself.

And why did you do?

Was having a laugh, I guess a faff.
  In speech he waffled and baffled.
He appeared daft, so I employed my craft.
  The events after, prompted my laughter.

So, what should he do?

His illness is not my business.

He is a mess, he only brings distress.
He is not fit to address, sighting him brings stress.
Let me guess, his living should be less.

Really! So, is that why you do? ‡

◆ 30.07.2012.

TWO VIEWS

There are two sides
  To every story,

A flip side
  To every glory,

A bright side
  To every worry,

An irretrievable side
  To every sorry!

A one-dimensional view
  Never the whole picture drew. ‡

  ♦ 10.08.2012.

HATE-HYPOCRISY

Imagine a hate that cannot relegate
  Its host, from the bait of its hate.

A hate that does elevate its hate
  From reprobate, to its hate alleviate.

Imagine a hate that does dissipate,
  Only to relate, by the demands of its hate.

How can your hate, your life regulate?
  Is your hate, your hate, or you, your hate? ‡

  ◆ 08.07.2013.

LAUGHED AT

Taunted for his seeming languid state,
  Clawed by outrage, to unguard his gate,
Defined and confined, to certify his fate,
  Still he does not yield to their bait.

Cheered and jeered, as his fall they await,
  Adjusting in disgust, as his person they hate,
Finalising their plans, they set a date,
  Still before him, their energies dissipate.

Considered minuscule, his flaws they equate,
  Then feign friendships, to their lies update,
With him they yarn, to prove him their candidate,
  Still his honesty, does them infuriate.

On and on, their theories they accentuate,
  Desperately wishing, to his burial officiate.
Working tirelessly, to his joys confiscate,
  Still grace does his heartbeat regulate. ‡

    ◆ 20.08.2012.

IDLE WORDS

Jest could be made,
  No harm intended.
But its showing most times,
  Has folly in attendance.
The intent of the heart,
  Isn't always comprehended.
Yet damages could last,
  Long after repentance.

It pays to be productive,
  Even in jest.
Take heed the expense,
  Despite the request.
Words are like seeds,
  And could hearts infest.
Complete mastery over the tongue,
  Is an ideal conquest.

In jest, intention is revealed,
  Attention's a thrill.
Condition might not be core,
  Information should be fore.

Pleasures can abound,

   But pressures may compound.

So, if jest is your decision,

   Be careful your incision. ‡

    ◆ 10.08.2012.

YOU BE! I WILL BE!

My every conversation,
  Instigates your investigations.
My every information,
  Exacerbates your insinuations.

Still you be! I will be!

My every glorification,
  Ignites your indignation.
My every recommendation,
  Slights your manipulation.

Still you be! I will be! ‡

  ◆ 14.08.2012.

LEAVE HIM BE

He is, he isn't
 Why the fuss?

Ask him, he'll tell
 What's your loss?

You spread, you tell
 What's your plus?

He lives, you live
 Is he your cuss? ‡

 ◆ 14.08.2012.

NEMESIS

The unrepentant wickedly condemn,
  While viewing their lives, as a royal diadem.
Quick to arbitrate, glimpsing no gem,
  Joyous that it's never about them.

But in a moment,
  They are deracinated by their stem.
And overwhelmed,
  Becomes their riotous emblem. ‡

  ◆ 05.10.2012.

BOY

Nameless, clueless
    He is imbibing.

Picking up tendencies,
    He is climbing.

Responding, upholding
    He is vibing,

To the subscriptions and inscriptions
    Paraded by his custodians. ‡

    ◆ 14.04.2013.

CURRICULUM VITAE

My life exemplifies a slimy swamp.
  Clogged up by decomposing matter.
Perfumed by nauseating toxins,
  I am a reproach in all environs.
My 'friends' flee from me, I radiate gloom.
  Men detest my presence, I know no essence.
I am secluded, excluded, polluted, and deluded.

Futuristically,
  I am an epitome of blindness.
My folly is substantiated by her produce –
  A life marred by abysmal benefits.

Heinous are my qualifications –
  A veteran in the field of hypocrisy.
Euphoric inspirations geared by selfishness.
  A frame contoured by gluttony.
An expert at perversion's detection.
  A passion driven by emotional tides.
A collector of humiliation and shame.

How can You have a job for me friend?

As You can see, I only qualify for doom.

Yes! You are the prime
  candidate for my transformation.
The only payment I demand of you is faith —
  Any deposit is guaranteed to suffice. ‡

  ◆ 04.10.2008.

LATENT TALENT

Many men sit wondering,
  What they could their world give.
Yet, void of earthly orderings,
  Huge talents within their hearts, live.

That you'll explore,
  I implore.
Please do not detour,
  Let blessings recur.

Many men sit wondering,
  What they could their world give.
These many should quit bothering,
  And release their geniuses, to live.

With your grandeur,
  I do concur.
So, give us some more,
  Let your heart's grace, pour. ‡

  ◆ 22.12.2008.

BLANK

Discerning this narrow! Blank!
  Containing this sorrow! Blank!
Maintaining my barrow! Blank!
  Concerning tomorrow! Blank!

  Blank!
  Blank! Blank!

Please Lord speak to me! Blank!
  Please Lord help me see! Blank!
Please Lord who is me! Blank!
  Please Lord I'll agree! Blank!

  Blank!
  Blank! Blank!

Will these tears ever dry? Blank!
  Contemplating why! Blank!
Curse God and die! Blank!
  Trust God still try! Blank!

  Blank!

Blank! Blank! ‡

♦ 08.05.2013.

IN SANITY

My character's assassination by you,
  Breeds social contamination, true,
Which is both contagious and perilous,
  Hence shame frames my name.

        I should remain sane!

My character's redefinition by me,
  Contemplates a social intimidation, or two,
Which are both noxious and insidious,
  Hence patience licenses my silence.

        Though my mind's insane!

My character's annihilation by them,
  Festers my social deterioration anew,
Which is both injurious and cancerous,
  Hence play strays to grey.

        Should I remain sane?

My character's rehabilitation by me,

Demands a social modification so due,
Which is both emotive and expensive,
Hence stance's distance in this instance.

I will remain sane! ‡

◆ 25.07.2012.

UNDYING TRY

In this time of why,
  God sees that we cry.
Again, His grace He'll apply,
  To more than the tears, dry.
That we may like eagles, fly.

So, though we only hurt espy,
  And our grief makes us wry.
Such that all of life seems to die,
  And laughter puts on shy.
Remember, God's nigh.

He is Lord of all that's high,
  He is intimate with that sigh,
On His love, we can helplessly rely.
  For it will never say "Goodbye!"
That's why, we'll still try. ☦

  ◆ 30.03.2013.

BREAK ME

Break me oh Lord!
Let this heart hardened
  By hurts, be molten.
Let the tears freely flow,
  From my love for You.
Let my heart continually,
    Yearn for You.

Break me oh Lord!
Let the path of unrighteousness,
  Nauseate my entirety.
Let my hunger for You override,
  These fleeting pleasures.
Let our discourse always be,
    Indispensable to me.

Break me oh Lord!
To the point where all
  Of me reflects Your grace.
To the point where my solitary
  Satisfaction is You.
To the point where my

Identity, is You.

For how can I love You,
Save for brokenness? ‡

◆ 25.08.2008.

YET BOUND

The flaws I see,
  Floor many laws
That govern success.

The stores I see,
  Draw even whores
That ration access.

The wars I see,
  Gnaw at the doors
That beckon fortress.

The shores I see,
  Claw at the jaws
That suction excess. ‡

  ◆ 06.02.2013.

HE SANK, I SANK

He drank and drank,
  As his dreams sank and sank,
Lies stole his rank,
  Failures emptied his bank.

He drank and drank,
  Till his personality stank.
He was labelled a crank,
  Though men knew he was frank.

He drank and drank,
  Numbing the pain in his tank,
Yearning to be blank,
  Such that he dreaded to any thank.

He drank and drank,
  As his failures did him flank.
Before me he stank,
  But even then, I sank. ‡

  ◆ 25.11.2012.

FETTERED FETTERS

Newsflash! Flashy
  Is now tantamount to trashy.
Subtle evasions
  Trail disdainful stance.
Sarcasm humours,
  Seeking to confer great turmoil.
My approach, men scrutinise.
  I do escape, conceptualise.

I won't, for any man
  Who studies to proclaim flaws,
Is elusive to his clan
  Of internally resident outlaws!

Motioned by notions,
  My options all seem auctioned.
Comedy beckons tragedy
  As she reckons my mockery.
Surrounding movements
  seeks to murder my improvements.
now the criticisms,
  Flourish within myopia.

Certainly, imperfection
  Is guaranteed from all humanity.
Conquests in education
  Give no immunity to this vulnerability! ‡

  ◆ 22.07.2012.

HOPELESS HOPE

What hope is there?
  For a man who does nothing but curse,
For him who cannot goodness nurse,
  For him who forever hides his purse.

What hope is there?
  For the man who has lost his cause,
For the man who's living on pause,
  For the man who commands no applause.

What hope is there?
  For a man who is filled with faults,
For a man daily torn by insults,
  For a man loaded with disdainful halts.

What hope is there?
  Jesus Christ is near. ‡

    ◆ 10.12.2012.

HONESTY

Honesty values truth's sovereignty
  Way above any of life's pending cemetery.
Wickedness ills her own longevity,
  With investments from hell's repository.

When wickedness sights displayed honesty,
  She yells out loud — "That's pedantry!"
For she always seeks to beat integrity,
  With unfounded, but guarded effrontery.

Yet wisdom — honesty's defense, does guarantee
  Immunity, to any abusive dignitary.
Her parties eliminate peasantry,
  Her ardour unveils an Eternal Royalty. ✝

  ◆ 03.04.2013.

LORD WHAT CAN YOU DO?

The man said —
Lord what can You do with stupid?
  What can You do with insipid?
Lord what can You do with horrid, torrid?
  What can You do with me?

The Lord said — Wait and see!

The man said —
Lord what can You do with conflicted?
  What can You do with he who inflicted — pain?
Lord what can You do with convicted, evicted?
  What can You do with me?

The Lord said — Wait and see!

The man said —
Lord what can You do with blind?
  What can You do with a sinful mind?
Lord what can You do with defined, unrefined?
  What can You do with me?

The Lord said — Wait and see! ‡

- ✦ 18.04.2013.

WAIT

Ensue lucid comprehension,
  Eschew hurried communication,
Subdue torrid irritation.
  For man's justification
Does not birth God's glorification.[3] ‡

  ◆ 13.04.2013.

---

[3] *Remixing* James 1:19 -20

GOING THROUGH

Isolated! Yes, but
  My strength is documented.

Irritated! Yes but
  My brilliance is accentuated.

Emaciated! Yes, but
  My mind is educated.

Regulated! Yes but
  My focus is elevated.

In time, this would be a past
  That my growth, did outlast. ‡

  ◆ 21.12.2012.

PSALMS 23 (REVISED)

1 The Self-Existent One
  Associates with me as friend,
I shall not decrease,
  Fail, lessen or have need.

2 He grants me
  Recumbency and incumbency
In habitations supple
  With fresh nourishment.
He gently leads me on,
  Beside living and resting waters.

3 Refocusing and realigning
  My life's intent and content with His.
He propels my motion in the way
  Of His expectations of me,
For His own purpose
  — A manifestation of His glory through me.

4 So though I proceed
  Through the alleys and valleys
Of death or through sin's

Consequential and detrimental depth,
I will revere no fierceness,
   Harshness or wildness.
For God is with me, His authority
   And his sustenance, renew my strength.

5 He sets in order
   Then organises a meal for me,
In front of my seeming distress and oppressors.
   He takes away the ashes from my head,
With His soothing richness,
   My containers abound with His
Overflowing fullness.

6 Certainly, Cod's covenantal
   Devotion to showing His strength,
Steadfastness and love to His own,
   Pursues after me with intention
To overtake and overcome me
   For all my lifetime,

I am settled in the sanctuary
   Of the Self-Existent One
Without limits! Perpetually! ‡

◆ 29.05.2013.

FUNCTIONING SILENCE

Silence! Still the workings reveal You,
  Engaging in my every being, via seeming nothings.
Florescence finds her way to my true,
  Expunging my fallings with her fountains.

I didn't adjure or conjure,
  I survived another ill-fated seizure.

Silence! Still my stockings unveil You,
  Arranging my every being, via new promptings.
Effervescence does my being pursue,
  Foraging for gems humming on my mountain.

I didn't conjure or adjure,
  I contrived in another ill-fated seizure.

Silence, but my pluckings up sale You,
  Changing my every being via deeming routings.
Convalescence invades my avenue,
  Rummaging and expelling dirt to aid sprouting.

I didn't conjure or adjure,

I arrived at my God-ordained pleasure. ‡

♦ 17.06.2013.

GOD'S COMMITMENT

I love you,
So, I'm involved with you
   To prosper you and bring you to that end
Which I had already destined for you,
   Before the foundations of the world.

I disturb you,
To be perturbed by sameness
   My grace is enough to alter any place
Which man's institution holds true.
   There is no limitation in My world.

I nourish you,
For flourish is your due
   It is treason if you cannot another, season.
Ditch man's definition of you,
   For awe's inspiration gave you to the world.

I train your
Mind to reign with you
   My purpose in you will vain altars dispose.
Switch to My Word to enlighten your view,

And we'll show your glory, to the world. ‡

♦ 02.02.2013.

SQUEEZED

My treasures pressured my pain
I camouflaged in love, to feed my wanting
For acceptance.

Your pressures pleasure my gain
Counting flaws, would leave me panting –
Hence repentance.

I ensure the detour's no more
By surmounting doubts instead of ranting.
Now endurance. ‡

◆ 20.08.2011.

FAITH AND DOINGS

Sporadic ridicules,
  Pedantic obstacles,
Psychotic graticules,
  Nomadic vehicles.

These are
  Functioning my faith.

Unexplained extensions,
  Postponed evictions,
Cancelled retributions,
  Paralleled distributions.

These are
  Functioned by my faith. ‡

  ◆ 21.07.2013.

NO INSULT

There's no insult you can invent,
  That will result in my torment.

Nor is there an insult which you can invent,
  Yet to seek my assault as its key event.

Nor an insult which you'll invent,
  That can default my content.

For Christ is my default, he died to me exalt,
  It's Him that I'll consult, in Him I live,
                    move and be. ‡

  ◆ 06.05.2013.

STRANGER TO MYSELF

Stranger to myself,
  My mirror presents a strange me.
I project defiance but this is
  An inflicted conflict, an afflicting verdict.
  But my mind's privy to another levy.

Danger to myself,
  My mirror presents a strange me.
I inject buoyance but this is
  A dejected reject, a subjecting object.
  Still my mind's privy to another levy.

Stranger to myself,
  My mirror presents a changed me.
I accept compliance and this is
  A forfeited orbit, a conceiting summit.
  Yes! My mind's privy to order's levy! ‡

  ◆ 19.06.2013.

DOUBT

Hello, how are you?
  Conversation.

Excuse me, see you later!
  Trepidation.

Back to position, same duty,
  Relegation.

Smiling, piling, yet
  Denigration.

Fickleness, still I laugh
  Declaration —

  "It's for my good
  I need not brood!" ‡

  ◆ 10.08.2012.

FUNNY

Funny how you are loathed for a lie,
  Never confirmed years down the line,
The vicious rumour should make you die,
  Yet His story, causes you to shine.

  Within is a savour,
    Which hate cannot flavour,
  My only endeavour,
    Is to spot God's armour – love.

Funny how you can be so different,
  From the cause of the rumour's current,
Only grace can make me so fluent,
  In love, in spite of hatred's intent.

  Within is a savour,
    Which hate cannot flavour,
  My only endeavour,
    Is to spot God's armour – love.

Funny how they crowd and wait,
  Thinking they can truth abate,

Only to have their truth equate,
  To a folly so very great. ‡

  ◆ 24.05.2013.

UNLINK

When you break sin's link,
  Be sure not to wink or blink,

Neither drink nor even think
  To ink, the kink of that link,

For that brink will stink,
  Of evil's slink, and you shrink.

None of sin's chink or clink
  Should govern your link.[4] ‡

♦ 27.03.2013.

---

[4] Re: Isaiah 43.18 – Remember not the former things, nor consider the things of old.

FAITH-HOLD

Every God given prophecy
  Advertises the enemy's redundancy,
So, he baits with his currency –
  Reasons to God doubt.

Sinuously working to avert due residency,
  The designed recipient's occupancy,
And God's inalterable ascendancy –
  He plots to faith, clout.

So, shun ostensible despondency
  Glory in God's supremacy
As He augments your legacy –
  Make His praise your shout. ✝

  ◆ 30.04.2013.

GIANT STRIDES

Exceeding limitation, denying confirmation,
  Provoking negotiation, evading relaxation.

Arriving destination, compelling proclamation,
  Surviving elimination, igniting motivation.

Highlighting elevation, neglecting condemnation,
  Forgetting humiliation, believing revelation.

Irrefutably proven,
  I take giant, gargantuan strides. ✝

◆ Written in 2001.

SCANDAL TO SANDAL

Mistakes were made, the price is being paid,
   Enough is never said, vultures have preyed.

      Scandal – but Jesus forgave.

Price has been paid, enough is never said,
   Culture has been greyed, vultures are stayed.

      Sandal – New ones, Jesus gave.

Both desire to rule, one inspires my rule,
   Revealing is this sandal's healing, despite scandal. ✝

  ◆ 27.05.2013.

MESSED UP, DRESSED UP

Nothing outdoes having
  Messed up, dressed up.

Transformation intertwines
  Messed up and dressed up.

God is faithful to your
  Messed up, dress up.

I treasure the journey between
  Messed up and dressed up. ‡

  ◆ 13.02.2013.

WAITING FOR SHE

Longing for a talk that would birth oneness
Not necessarily from our vision's sameness
But as a result of the Almighty God's prowess
Intimating in me a 'two become one' wholeness. ‡

◆ 13.01.2013.

GRACE

Justice is deserved,
　　But now not served,
Cruel intents are reserved,
　　Even now, not preserved.

For payback-time collapses,
　　As faith encompasses.
The revenue of grace surpasses
　　Justice. Reprisal bypasses. ‡

　◆ 15.04.2013.

INTENSE

Impulsed by the beam of a stare,
   I turn towards the direction of its source,
Our eyes meet, I turn away,
   The game begins — thence to.

For the rest of our 'meet' we shyly observe,
   If we are still being scrutinised by the other,
Should the game go on,
   Or should we graduate — hence to?

Finally, we exit our togetherness,
   No words said, just looks, bland looks,
I return to my busyness,
   Wondering — whence to. ‡

   ◆ 07.10.2011.

BE GRATEFUL

Your gratitude,
  To your miracle,
Plays the altitude,
  Of your oracle.

In the magnitude
  Of your pinnacle,
Render servitude,
  Despite the cubicle. ‡

  ◆ 27.09.2011.

ALL THIS

Lord I thank You —
   For this! My this!
   In this! With this!

Lord I thank You —
   From this! To this!
   And this! Through this!

Lord I thank You —
   By this! On this!
   Off this! I'll replay this! ‡

   ◆ 24.04.2013.

MY SHEPHERD

Conceptually inexplicable,
  Were the workings of You
Which ensured regulation,
  And abjured speculation.
Tilting confirmations towards fallacy,
  As Your revelations shambled my heresy,
Hence taming my braggadocious,
  And flaming the inauspicious.

Conceptually indelible are
  The workings of You,
Which secure affirmation
  And procure elevation.
All my learning meet an impasse,
  All my yearning cannot surpass,
The tangibility of Your sleuth,
  The durability of Your truth. ‡

   ◆ 11.06.2013.

WAS DEAD

I was dead! Dead to
 The brutality of my sins.
I was dead! Dead to
 My hostility towards God.

 White lies, foul cries
  Sensual highs, slander's ties.

I was dead! At great
 Commonality with all sins.
I was dead! Dead to my
 Acerbity towards God.

 Ever incessant,
  Never ever repentant! ‡

 ◆ 13.08.2013.

ON LOVE

The occurrence of any prophecy,
  In independence from smouldering currency,
Amounts to nothing without love.

If I demystify all mysteries,
  And beauty all elementaries,
It amounts to nothing without love.

My demonstration of eloquence,
  In and beyond every location of earthly influence,
Amounts to nothing without love.

If we certify poverty's elimination,
  And clarify every misconception,
It amounts to nothing without love.

Though my courteousness be infectious,
  And my ableness be unpretentious,
It amounts to nothing without love.[5] ‡

---

[5] A poetic rendition of 1 Corinthians 13: 1-3.

◆ 12.02.2013.

DESPAIR

What love do you have knowing that
   The Author of the universe is against you,

Knowing that your every action is
   Indicative of deeds which He abhors,

Understanding that your dreams are
   Nothing but avenues for self-glorification,

Seeing that your perversity
   Results from nothing but your iniquity? ‡

   ◆ 04.09.2008.

LOVE IS DIVINE

Only Divine Sovereignty,
  Can love before physicality.
For every human's conditionality,
  Has an already determined finality — death!

All of humanity,
  Can only love truly, via Divinity.
Else it is all based on a desired connectivity,
  With a potential credibility — lust! ‡

  ◆ 23.05.2013.

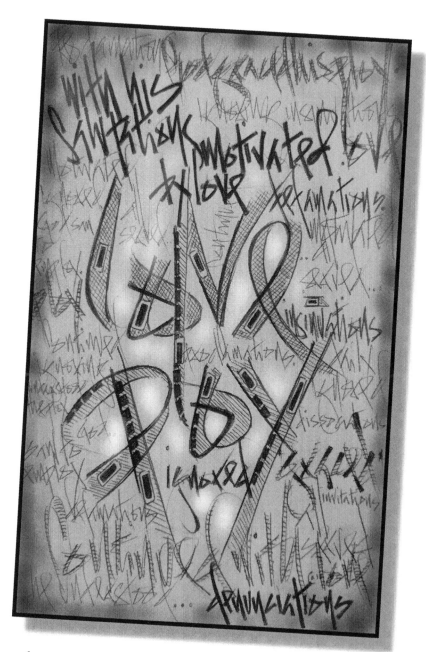

LOVE-PLOY

Daily ignored, he understood the ploy.
  Daily ignored, he understood his ploy.

He continued with his salutations, dedications,
  Proclamations, and invitations, motivated by love.

Daily ignored, he understood the ploy.
  Daily ignored, God saw to employ.

He continued, ignoring insinuations, defamations,
  Dissociations, and denunciations, motivated by love.

Daily ignored, God graced his ploy.
  Daily ignored, all served God's ploy. ‡

  ◆ 07.05.2013.

LOVE'S DOING

Love makes me
  Forgive and not relive
The acrimonies
  Wielded by youthful blunder.

Love makes me
  Conceive and then achieve
The testimonies
  Wielded by dutiful surrender. ‡

  ◆ 17.08.2013.

LORD, I COME!

Lord, I come!
Through the wary eyes of suspicion,
  Through the venom of slander,
Through the flees of disdain,
  Through the heights of ridicule, I come!

Lord, I come!
With self-esteem beneath infinitesimal,
  Cumbered by edginess sourced by paranoia,
Wanting for a hearing far-fetched,
  So unsure of the perceptions all around, I come!

Lord, I come!
Not trusting my boundaries,
  Still shackled to the same old circumference,
Sceptical about my every inference,
  Disbelieving my every expectation, I come!

Still, I come!
  Knowing You are bigger than all, I come! ‡

  ◆ 09.11.2008.

OBEDIENCE

Your stay is my stay,
  Today, every day.
Your go is my go,
  This low is no low.

My obedience channels a flow,
  From springs of wisdom, never slow.
By this, the pearls of greatness around me glow,
  And I'm warned of any harmful blow.

Your give is my live,
  I did receive, so I believe.
Your seed is my heed,
  That weed, may not breed.

My obedience flavours my school,
  With recipes unknown to the fool.
The abundance, equals no pool.
  The contents, know no drool.

Your cool is my tool,
  To rule and to fuel.

Your will is my pill,
  To still and to drill.

My obedience sections me from disease,
  And estranges my heart from decease.
She guarantees the faithful release,
  Of heaven's eternal bliss.

Lord, Your way is my way,
  Come what may, I won't stray.
Your view remains my view,
  For there is a new, in all that's due. ‡

◆ 25.02.2013.

DEUTERONOMY 28:1–14.

In transaction, production,
  reproduction, cultivation,
declaration and distribution.

  I am blessed because
  I diligently obey the Lord.

In participation, sanctification,
  optimisation, galvanisation,
globalisation and authorisation.

  I am blessed because
  I diligently obey the Lord.

In multiplication, illumination,
  confiscation, denunciation,
acquisition, fortification.

  I am blessed because
  I diligently obey the Lord. ‡

  ◆ 27.02.2013.

WISDOM

Wisdom is not classy,
  Hence the proud unwittily pass.
She is not bossy,
  Therefore, fools unwittily curse.

But those who perceive her,
  Ultimately receive her.
Though all could conceive of her,
  Who can deceive her?

Wisdom is not flashy,
  But with man's societal laws, she'll clash.
She may seem very trashy,
  But all her oppositions, crash.

Those who engage her,
  Uncage her in their age.
And those who estrange her,
  Are the sacrilege of their age.

Wisdom could appear marshy
  But she is way tougher than brass.

If you ever think her ashy,
  Then, from you she'll pass. ‡

  ◆ 09.05.2013.

OLD WOMAN

I once met an old woman
  At the marketplace.

She was —
Wisened by age, toughened by life.
  Enlightened by education, silenced by meditation.
Tanned by the sun, respected by *some* passers-by.
  Delighted by activity...

But most of all, admired by me! ‡

  ◆ Written before 2000.

Time is a gift depreciating on every count.
   Ultimately, she will demand for your account,
Then you'll have to all your progresses recount.
   Eternal achievements know no discount. ‡

◆ 22.09.2012.

INDEX OF POEM TITLES

Printed in Poland
by Amazon Fulfillment
Poland Sp. z o.o., Wrocław

59811078R00092